Reiki and Christian Beliefs: Where Do They Intersect?

An invitation to learn about Reiki, a hands-on healing modality, ancient Christian Beliefs and their common ground.

SARAH C. STOCKHAM

Copyright © 2017 Sarah C. Stockham
All rights reserved.

ISBN: 1543242952
ISBN 13: 9781543242959
Library of Congress Control Number: 2017902721
CreateSpace Independent Publishing Platform
North Charleston, South Carolina

QUOTES

[Jesus] said to her, "Daughter, your faith has healed you. Go in peace and be freed from your suffering."

Mark 5:34

"Reiki is experiential; so is peace."

Michael Stockham

"You hem me in behind and before, and you lay your hand upon me. Such knowledge is too wonderful for me."

Psalm 139:5-6

All Bible quotations are from The Holy Bible, New International Version,
Copyright © 1978 by New York International Bible Society.

FOREWORD

When I first attuned Sarah to Reiki, Levels 1 & 2, she immediately connected the dots between Reiki and her own Christian beliefs. She has fully embraced Reiki and uses it in her daily life and has continuously studied Reiki as it relates to Christianity and also personal healing. As a Reiki Master, she is so passionate about sharing Reiki with others and using Reiki to help and heal. A Reiki session with Sarah is powerful, yet gentle, healing and relaxing. Sarah creates a safe, non-judgmental environment, which promotes deeper relaxation and healing.

Janice Berkenheger
Certified Holistic Health and Transformational Coach
www.JaniceBerkenheger.com

DEDICATION

The intention of this book is to create a protected space—based on a solid spiritual foundation, surrounded and walled by experiences—where we can have a conversation about Reiki (pronounced "ray-key"), a hands-on healing modality. I am opening a dialogue. I do not necessarily think all who engage in the conversation will give Reiki a try. However, if this conversation causes you to look for ways to destress, pursue healing, create a personal space for quiet reflection, or engage in a new modality for a conversation with the Divine, then I will consider the time spent writing to be highly valuable.

This book is dedicated to all who seek healing:

spiritual
mental
emotional
physical
social

May you be deeply blessed on your journey, so that you may then gratefully light the way for another.

ACKNOWLEDGEMENTS

Thank you, Mike, for choosing me on this journey we call life! Thank you for encouraging me and listening as I wonder aloud.

Morgan Elaine, the journey you have provided me as a parent has been an awakening. Your thought process continues to help me grow in maturity, and as a writer.

Thank you, Doug and Elaine Crowder, ("Uncle Doug" and "Aunt Elaine" to hundreds; Dad and Mom to me) for your constant prayers over my life. From my unexpected conception as the African drums of war were beginning, to my need at birth for extra care, to widening my community of impactful conversations and encouragement [French word that literally means "to press courage into the heart"], to blessing my decision to choose a far different path than my medically gifted sisters. Thank you for living your unwavering belief in "God is our refuge and strength, an ever-present help in trouble."—from the ancient Hebrew hymnal Psalms chapter 46:1—and teaching all to "Trust in the Lord with all your heart, and lean not on your own understanding. In all your ways submit to him, and he will make your paths straight" Proverbs 3:5-6.

William Lee Rand, thank you for fully embracing Usui / Holy Fire II Reiki and authoring many books on Reiki, including <u>Reiki, the Healing Touch</u>. Taking classes with you continues to redefine for me the capacity of "Reiki is love" concept. Thank you for reading my manuscript and suggesting important clarifications.

Thank you, Beth Misner, author of <u>Jesus and the Secret,</u> for having the vision and passion to found the Journey Center, Claremont, and for asking me to join the book club.

Janice Berkenheger, Thank you for sharing openly at the Journey Center, Claremont book club. The discussion on mediation truly changed me. Thank you for offering to share Reiki with me, and for being my first Reiki Master.

I am deeply grateful to each who engaged in thought provoking discussions, made me clarify my thinking in this writing process, and, or shared Reiki stories for me to include: Mike Stockham, Morgan Stockham, Janice Berkenheger, Carol Montgomery, LMFT, Kaitlyn Swift, Tracie Fiore, Lori J. Paley, Michele Hernandez, Beth Kummerle, Reverend Karen Sapio, Kumud Bothra, Tom Hallberg, Beth Huey-Levine, Patricia Scott, and the Reiki Claremont Reiki Share 2016 family.

My heart is full.

Dear Reader,

Feel free to jump around, or read straight through. It is a small book divided into five sections. You might be able to read Parts 1-3 in one sitting. Part 4 and 5 are for those who are interested in my journey and what's next at Reiki Claremont.

~Sarah

CONTENTS

Quotes	iii
Foreword	v
Acknowledgements	ix
Part One: Reiki	1
1 What is Reiki?	3
2 Reiki Stories	7
3 Reiki Benefits	15
4 Reiki History: Usui to Holy Fire II	19
5 An Invitation to a Place of Calm	23
Part Two: Where Do Reiki and Christian Beliefs Intersect?	29
6 Nicene Creed	31
7 Where Reiki and Christian Beliefs Intersect	35
8 Reiki and Anointing with Oil	39
9 Reiki and Source of Healing	41
10 Where Reiki and Jesus's Healing Ministry Intersect	43
11 Where Reiki, Prayer and Symbols Intersect	49
12 Reiki and King David's Declaration	53
13 More of Where Reiki and Christian Beliefs Intersect	57

Part Three: Reiki Claremont		59
14	About Reiki Claremont ~an invitation to learn~	61
15	What to Expect in a Reiki Session	63
16	Reiki in Use	67
Part Four: My Road to Usui / Holy Fire II Reiki		73
17	What's in a Name?	75
18	Protected!	77
19	The Book Club	83
20	Holy Fire II Reiki	85
21	How Did my Reiki Placement Change Me?	87
Part Five: Conclusion in Two Parts		91
22	Conclusion	93
23	What's Next?	95

PART ONE: REIKI

...

1
WHAT IS REIKI?

The National Institutes of Health's (NIH) National Center for Complementary and Alternative Medicine (NCCAM) shares *"Reiki is a complementary health practice in which practitioners place their hands lightly on or just above the person, with the goal of facilitating the person's own healing response."* This book is about finding the common ground between Reiki and Christian beliefs. The Bible share many examples of healing. Reiki is hands-on healing. Where do the two healing modalities intersect?

I was raised in a Christian home where fact based, scientific discussions were common. When I was introduced to Reiki, I had many questions. As I studied both the practice of Reiki and Ancient Scriptures, I began to find parallels and connections. This book is written to specifically address Reiki and Christian beliefs as a layperson.

Reiki (pronounced "ray-key") is a compound word. Rei in Hebrew means "my shepherd"; in Japanese it means "spirit". Ki means "life energy". All living things have energy. There is a point of view that supports when a person's life energy, or Ki, is weakened, a person looks pales, withdrawn. Conversely, when someone is full of life, or their Ki is strong, they are full of energy, vibrant. I experience Reiki as an invitation to blessing and healing from life's divine source, God/Jesus/Holy Spirit.

Reiki is not a religion. Like electricity, the energy we, or our bodies, create flows and is measureable. Like gravity, Reiki is an unseen force. Reiki encourages the body to relax and find balance, allowing the body to heal itself. Reiki does not replace western medicine; like yoga and deep breathing, it complements it. You can be of any religious affiliation, or none, and still benefit from electricity. You can be of any religious affiliation, or none, and benefit from Reiki.

As there are different denominations in the Christian church, there are different styles of Reiki. The different denominations occurred over interpretation and application. In some respects the different styles of Reiki also naturally developed along similar lines. The soft, gentle style of Usui / Holy Fire II Reiki is the one I am clearly thinking of when writing.

REIKI AND CHRISTIAN BELIEFS: WHERE DO THEY INTERSECT?

Some will say there is an unknown spiritual component of Reiki, and to be wary of it. A component of "spiritual" is sensing something bigger than self, and "faith" is believing in something bigger than self. Since Usui / Holy Fire II Reiki comes from Creator/Source (something bigger than me), then, yes, you could say there is a spiritual component; but I also have faith God/Jesus/Holy Spirit is the source of Peace, and of healing. My experience with God/Jesus/Holy Spirit in my Reiki practice is One who is all forgiving, compassionate, welcoming with healing; not vengeful or harsh.

Is it possible for people with ego centric agendas to practice Reiki? Of course it is. It is wise to prayerfully consider who is touching you and what their intent is. Feel free to ask about their Reiki practice. If at any point you feel uncomfortable, speak up! If you have ever experienced Divine peace and love, you'll know if the source of energy is malicious or Good.

All, regardless of their spiritual beliefs, also use gravity, and electricity—other unseen forces that are present on Earth. I believe, since gravity and electricity have been studied more in depth over a longer period of time, there is both a broader understanding of them and their uses to better our lives. Someday, I hope science will develop more sensitive methods for measuring the biofield, the energy our bodies produce. I think that will help Reiki become more main stream.

Hands-on healing comes in many forms and modalities. Some use "kangaroo mother" touch for preemies to increase prognosis. Some choose massage to clear the lymph system. Others take salt scrubs or Epsom salt soaks followed by rinsing the skin and applying essential oils. Jesus's biographers shared several instances where he used hands-on healing.

The practice of hand-on healing is ancient; hands-on healing named Reiki is a newer labeling, if you prefer. Reiki, born out of a culture of meditation and quiet, is a gentle practice that seeks to help the body move towards balance, and thus facilitate faster healing.

So, are there similarities and, perhaps commonalities, between the practice of hands-on healing modality of Reiki, and Jesus's form of hands-on healing? How about some testimonials to give a better view of what Reiki can do?

2

REIKI STORIES

The following stories are shared by people across America who have found Reiki to not only be a great tool for relaxation, but also for different types of healing, both personal and for others. Each person is Reiki trained.

■ ■ ■

Through my practice of Reiki, I have found the way to hear the voice of God through the voice of Reiki. For me, they are one and the same. My understanding can be found in the very meaning of the word Reiki: the Japanese character for Rei may be translated as *spirit consciousness, God consciousness, the Supreme being;* the ki as *energy of life*. I have learned to listen to Reiki's voice--to trust it, to follow its guidance and surrender to the changes that I have had to make. As a result, my life has been transformed to one of bliss and peace. Reiki heals our lives on all levels if we willingly follow the voice of Reiki and work on our problems. Knowing that God wants only the highest good for me has made it easier to surrender and change. I know that I am on the right path for my life when I follow Reiki's guidance.

Reiki can heal our overall being, right into our core, as it heals on all levels: physical, mental, emotional and spiritual. But to do this, we must be prepared not only to take Reiki in but also to release our bad habits and this requires that we make changes. With Reiki to guide us on our right path, we can make these changes and begin to make the right decisions on all levels. This then assists us in our transformation process, healing us so that we are better able to help others through the voice of Reiki.

Kumud Bothra
Director
Reiki India in association with William
Lee Rand and the International Center for
Reiki Training
Holy Fire II Karuna Reiki Representative
in India

Excerpt from "Learning to Hear the Voice of Reiki" article published in (c) Reiki News Magazine, Fall 2016, p.13 www.reiki.org. Used with permission.

■ ■ ■

Having been an esthetician and providing skin care for clients for over 20 years, I think I've finally found the one thing that truly rounds out the treatments I provide for my guests in my facial room. Many years ago, I came to realize that providing an expert facial is more than just the "steam and cream" aspect of the treatment. When caring for my clients, I've known that it's important to care for the whole person, and not just the facial skin that is under my hands. After receiving my Reiki training and certification, I've been infusing Reiki techniques into my facial treatments. It has been eye-opening to see a profound difference in my client's response to their facials. Clients tend to fall asleep more frequently now and they are more rested and calm when they leave. New clients have been more apt to rebook, the energy in my spa and on the part of my staff has shifted to be even more positive, and it seems to be growing our business. I believe clients leave me and my spa in a better place mentally and physically after they receive a facial that is infused with the elements of Reiki.

Lori J. Paley
Owner of Aromatique Skin & Body Care
Claremont, CA

■ ■ ■

I was born into a devoutly religious, Irish-Catholic family in which Sunday mass was a weekly requirement as was fasting before partaking of the blessed Eucharist. Growing up, my mother taught myself and my siblings how to pray while kneeling at our bedside. Years later, my paternal grandmother taught me how to pray the Holy Rosary; to put my faith and trust in Jesus and His mother the Blessed Virgin, Mary. The ability to pray to and have faith in a God that loves us so much that He allowed His only son to die in order to absolve our sins was never lost on me. It's an amazing story of love and forgiveness that deeply moved me so much that I considered attending seminary schools for those interested in entering the priesthood both in high school and college. It was only a stronger yearning to marry and one day have a family that ultimately, took me on a different path away from becoming a priest.

At 28, with a two-year-old son and another on the way, I still was feeling the call to aid others; to help and to heal myself and others in some way that my career didn't allow me to fulfill. It was then I began to search my faith and the metaphysical sciences. Yet, it wasn't until 10 years later, I was introduced to Reiki by my Mother. Being a true "doubting Thomas", I didn't believe in Reiki or "energy medicine" until I experienced it first hand at a training course some years later. There, being treated by others in a Reiki session, I experienced a tangible energy "high" and peace that I had only experienced before in Church. It was; for me, proof that Reiki "worked". In both my self-practice and in treating others with Reiki, I know this healing modality really does help others in a multitude of ways: physical, emotional and spiritual healing being just the tip of the iceberg.

Religion is certainly something not everyone agrees with. But, whatever "faith" one chooses to follow, chances are it most likely is a deeply held, personal belief. I initially struggled with using Reiki to help others - some mentioned it being a sacrilege; among other things. It wasn't until I stumbled upon John 14:12 in a bible study class days after praying for guidance that I felt divinely led to the healing path of Reiki ("Truly, truly, I say to you, whoever believes in Me will also do the works that I do; and greater works than these will he do, because I am going to the Father.") After all, in Reiki, one believes the true healing comes from the Divine. In my Reiki practice, I pray to Jesus Christ and His Archangels to use me as a vessel for their holy work.

Now at 43, I still pray & converse daily with God. I attend Sunday mass and on occasion, morning mass and sometimes go late at night to sit in a Perpetual Adoration chapel to have quiet time alone with Christ. My wife and I have raised our children in the Catholic faith; and while I may not agree with every aspect of the Catholic Church, the basic tenants of love, compassion, forgiveness and faith are qualities our world still desperately needs and I believe in wholeheartedly. Reiki is something I believe serves those same principles, and furthermore allows me to introduce Jesus Christ to others that may not be of faith prior to meeting me for a Reiki session.

Whether it be meditation, yoga, reiki or the like I offer you this: If you find yourself searching for "more" in your life, trust that you are being led by something greater than yourself. Reserve your self-judgement, shut off your critical thinking and listen to your heart – it will not lead you astray.

> Tom Hallberg
> Usui / Holy Fire II Reiki Master & ICRT
> Associate Member

■ ■ ■

My first Reiki session was in Knoxville, TN when I was in my late 30's. A petite woman named Anna combined her studies of Maori tribal healing techniques with her Reiki and Shiatsu massage training. Not only did she assist in removing blocks in my energy centers and relieving my muscular discomfort in my shoulders and back, but she tapped into my IEF (Individual Energy Field) that opened my consciousness up to a new world of wonder and awareness of my self. I shed tears during our session, and the right side of my body tingled and quivered for a few minutes. This caught my attention and I asked her what was going on. As Anna gave me some tissues, she explained to me how the body can hold onto negative energies which create blocks in the body if they are not released. She assisted me in opening these blocked energies by applying Reiki and the techniques she learned while living with the Maori in New Zealand. She was the conduit where the Universal Life Force could enter and flow to where it was needed in order for me to heal and become rebalanced. I felt relaxed, rejuvenated and tingly afterwards. This was when the light bulb went on in my head and heart and I decided to pursue the Healing Arts with a passion.

As a Healing Arts professional, I am aware of the various modalities used for energy healing and the health benefits they bring to individuals, no matter what their religion, faith, or spiritual beliefs are in life. I was raised Christian and appreciate the foundation it gave me as I entered adulthood and began to explore all faiths. I found the healing power of prayer, meditation, setting intentions, and heart-centered service to others, as beneficial ways of self-care, but felt there was more to learn. As I studied, practiced, and researched, I realized the importance of caring for oneself, so that we can be of service to each other and share this healing energy with good health, clarity, balance, love and inner-peace. I am honored to be a Reiki Master and a certified Level 3 Healing Touch practitioner, and I give myself Reiki daily, so that I may be a healthy harmonious conduit for the Universal Life Force/God/Source/Great Mystery to flow through me, and assist others in their healing. Being of service to self and each other is a gift all of us can practice every day from any religious background in the world. Anna taught me more than she will ever know during my first Reiki session with her many years ago, and so have the multiple teachers I have had since that moment. Grateful to all I encounter on this journey of life.

Beth Huey-Levine
Usui / Holy Fire II Reiki Master

■ ■ ■

Holy Fire Reiki II is the most powerful tool I have for self-healing and healing those I love. What has surprised me has been that Reiki not only healed physical challenges but also emotional challenges. I have suffered with anxiety since I was a small child. Lying in bed one evening, after having given myself Reiki to heal inflammation in my hip, I rested my hands on my chest. I wasn't really thinking about healing my fear and anxiety but as I felt the warmth of Reiki flowing through my hands, I quickly realized what was happening. The intelligent energy of Reiki was going where it was needed, to my heart. After that night, I have given my heart Reiki regularly and my anxiety has vanished. I still feel fear when fear is appropriate, but no longer do I feel anxiety when in new situations or around new people.

I am noticing other changes as well—as I feel more confident generally, I'm not restless in meditation and I'm compassionately more available to other people. Reiki has been a welcome energy for healing my life.

Patricia Scott
Holy Fire Reiki II Master

■ ■ ■

3

REIKI BENEFITS

Here are some benefits I have seen with Reiki:

- Strengthened sense of well-being
- Effective, rapid de-stressor
- Increased sense of connection
- Experiences of inner peace, tranquility and stillness, refreshing the spirit
- Increased energy
- Rapid, decreased feelings of pain and anxiety
- Deeper, more restful nights of sleep [a few, as they move towards balance, experience vivid dreams at first]
- Deeper, more sustained state of balance
- Increased balance physically, mentally, emotionally, spiritually and socially

- Helpful in traversing deep loss
- Deeper sense of peace while gradually lessoning of crippling feelings of worry
- Broader sense of spiritual connectedness
- More willingness to be in community, rather than withdrawing
- Increased connection to unique creativity
- Increased awareness of untapped inner resources
- Increased digestion and natural pull towards foods and beverages that are better for individual
- Increased motivation
- Sense of relaxation
- Increased clarity; birds eye view of life to airplane view of life
- Increased intuition
- Increased sense of wholeness

Here are some things Reiki does NOT do:

- Take the place of medical or psychological treatment
- Negate a person's personal responsibility for their actions
- Treat those who do not want to be treated by Reiki; it respects free will.

Reiki, born out of a culture of meditation and quiet, is a gentle practice that seeks to help the body move towards balance, and thus facilitate faster healing. One can go to a Reiki practitioner and have a session, or learn to practice Reiki on themselves. A Reiki session often lasts between 15 and 90 minutes, depending on the client's wishes. The Reiki practitioner prepares the space and themselves prior to placing hands on a fully clothed clients head, neck, shoulders, abdomen, knees and feet; tissue is not manipulated. The recipient's "job" is to focus on breathing deeply and allow the body to down-shift, so to speak; to allow the right and left sides of the brain to communicate differently.

Research is starting to ask important questions as to how Reiki works. I believe part of what makes Reiki powerful as a practice to improve healing is our need as humans to be touched, to be noticed, to be. Additionally, finding an intentional, quiet, protected space gives permission to listen to ourselves. That is therapeutic. So is moving from one brain side dominance to bilateral brain problem solving.

4

REIKI HISTORY: USUI TO HOLY FIRE II

Dr. Mikao Usui, the founder of Usui styled Reiki, had little written about him. He was born in Japan in 1865 and died in 1926, and although not a medical doctor, was given the honorary title of Doctor. He sought to help people and tried several avenues. There were already four different Reiki schools in Japan when Usui went on a meditative retreat. While fasting and meditating, he experienced a life changing awareness. Rushing down the hill to tell others, he tripped on a root and hurt his toe. His immediate reaction was to cup his foot with his hands. The intense pain began to quickly subside. At first he was not sure what it meant. He realized the experience had awakened a knowledge, a paradigm shift, that Reiki, the gift of hands-on healing, can be awakened in everyone. Usui was given the opportunity to help many after an earthquake in 1923. The need was great. A friend and medical doctor, Dr. Chujiro Hayashi watched Usui work and began learning from him. Usui shared his knowledge freely with Dr. Hayashi. Usui encouraged Dr. Hayashi to continue to refine and change the way he taught Reiki. After Usui's death, Dr. Hayashi opened more clinics where Reiki practitioners could work with the ill. He began methodically keeping notes and standardizing hand placements and attunements, in Usui / Holy Fire II Reiki, called placements and ignitions.

A Reiki attunement is a prescribed method of connecting to the healing possibilities from God/Jesus/Holy Spirit. The healing connection, or awareness, was always available. But by choosing to study it and be attuned to it, it allows one to become an aware vessel. As a musician, I have my hand built baby grand piano professionally tuned prior to recitals. For many of the 88 notes on a piano, there are three strings that one hammer strikes when a note is played. Each string must be tuned to the same, preexisting vibration for the tuner to say the piano is in tune. Reiki training, along with the placement or ignition, enables one to access Reiki anytime, under any circumstance after one is "attuned" to the preexisting healing vibration.

We have Reiki in the West thanks to Mrs. Hawayo Takata. She lived in Hawai'i, and on a visit to her parents in Japan, went to Dr. Hayashi's clinic. Determined to learn all she could about Reiki, she devoted time to working with Dr. Hayashi. In 1938, after three years of training, she became one of only thirteen Reiki masters Dr. Hayashi trained. She brought her training back to the Hawai'i, and then to Canada and finally into America prior to her death in 1980. She trained 22 Reiki masters and continued to standardize the teaching process.

In following Usui's desire for our understanding of Reiki to change and therefore how Reiki is taught, William Lee Rand, using Tibetan influences, developed an Usui/Tibetan style of Reiki in 1989. It followed the Usui/Hayashi/Takata lineage. In 2014 he introduced the softer Usui / Holy Fire Reiki style, with easier attunements to Usui / Holy Fire II Reiki coming in late 2015. Holy Fire II allows the student to directly connect to God/Jesus/Holy Spirit's healing energy; the Reiki master merely provides the training and sets the table, so to speak. Holy Fire Reiki comes from Holy Spirit, with Jesus as its guide for how and when to use it.

What choices do you make to create a practice of space, of calm or quiet?

5

AN INVITATION TO A PLACE OF CALM

There is a place of calm—a quiet, refreshing, gently moving stream beside a cool, shade covered area. As you walk the green grass and you see a place to sit and take it all in. The sounds of water caressing the small boulders and pebbles, song birds conversing, wispy breeze in the trees makes you aware of this moment. There is something calling you to this place, this time of refreshing. Your attitude shifts from "human doer" to "human being"—alive in this moment. In this place of rest, you have a deep sense of knowing you have access to every tool you need for each part of your life: spiritual, intellectual, physical, relational, emotional, financial, and occupational.

There is something profound that happens when we make time for rejuvenating. Our cortisol levels drop as we breathe deeper, allowing more oxygenated blood to fill our beings. As the stress decreases, we start to see so many more parts, pieces, things touching our lives for which we can truly be thankful. As gratitude increases we see more possibilities of positive outcomes.

The acidic pace of our lives picks away at our mental wellbeing and we succumb to patterns of less sleep and more mood numbing actions: endless hours of screen time (monitors, phones…), thoughtless eating pounding down sugar, salt and simple carbs, rarely conversing for more than 2 minutes at a time with the people around us.

Research continues to validate that using both sides of the brain elevates our ability to problem solve and effectively strategize. This helps us cope with what life presents us. Using both sides of our brain helps us to problem solve better, and be generally happier and more fulfilled.

Tibetan monks spend hours a day in meditation. They intentionally remove themselves from many parts of society, limiting their intake of negative media, and processed foods. When researchers look for the best balanced, calm brains, often they site Tibetan monks—their daily lifestyle choices cause shifts in their brain that result in examples of happy, healthy brains. Is there a way to move towards a calm, happy, healthy brain? Without becoming a Tibetan monk? Is there ONE thing practiced daily that can help physiologically shift our brains towards healing balance? I believe there is: Reiki.

I believe we are created in ways we see and understand; our need food, shelter, water, to be in community… And I believe God created humans in ways we do not yet fully comprehend, the "unseen". I think there is a great deal of research to be done that will continue to shed light on many areas of our human bodies, especially the brain.

There is at times a great wall in church communities to resist anything we do not culturally or socially understand. I've seen this reluctance to even allow space for conversations by intelligent, spirit conscious believers to wonder out loud. Curiosity, even regarding laws and mechanisms God created, in some spiritual communities is scolded, frowned on.

I believe there are many practices we can engage in as Christ followers that will move us to a place of a physiologically more balanced brain. I believe prayer and meditation are included in this. I believe cultivating a practice of gratitude and thanksgiving can do wonders. I think playing brain games and being a life-long curious learner supports a healthy brain. I also believe Reiki can assist.

Because Reiki is experiential—you must experience it to have an understanding for a conversation—some are reluctant to try it.

I believe my relationship with God/Jesus/Holy Spirit is experiential. Many people shared their experiences with what God/Jesus/Holy Spirit Jesus had done for them; but it wasn't until I saw my own brokenness and knew there was healing available, that I "tried" God/Jesus/Holy Spirit.

I've also found some see their brokenness as their identity—and resist healing because it challenges what they know about themselves. They are miserable, but it is a known quantity that defines their being. Who would they be without that brokenness?

I believe Jesus used multiple modalities in his teaching and healing time on Earth. I am thankful for that! I am thankful one of his modalities was his use of healing touch. My experience is Reiki is one of many types of healing touch; massage is another. To my knowledge Jesus didn't use massage, but many, including Christians, know the healing benefits of massage and strategically use it in their self-care routine.

There is a place of calm—a quiet, refreshing, rejuvenating space. There is something calling you to this place, this time of refreshing. I invite you to be curious in your search for meaningful ways of self-care. I invite you to move towards a place of calm, a place of healing. I invite you to Holy Fire Reiki.

PART TWO: WHERE DO REIKI AND CHRISTIAN BELIEFS INTERSECT?

...

6

NICENE CREED

In 325 AD, Christian church leaders met to create a summary of the combined teachings in the 66 books which comprise the Bible. It is a succinct set of basic, commonly shared Christian beliefs. What they created is named the "Nicene Creed" because their meeting was in the Turkish city of Nicaea, (present day Iznik). This creed is the framework of our Christian beliefs, the tenants of our faith. Line four is of particular interest when discussing Reiki with Christians. Here is one translation of the complete Nicene Creed from the <u>Episcopal Church Book of Common Prayer</u> (1979):

We believe in one God,
the Father, the Almighty,
maker of heaven and earth,

of all that is, seen and unseen.
We believe in one Lord, Jesus Christ,
the only Son of God,
eternally begotten of the Father,
God from God, Light from Light,
true God from true God,
begotten, not made,
of one Being with the Father.
Through him all things were made.
For us and for our salvation
he came down from heaven:
by the power of the Holy Spirit
he became incarnate from the Virgin Mary,
and was made man.
For our sake he was crucified under
Pontius Pilate;
he suffered death and was buried.
On the third day he rose again
in accordance with the Scriptures;
he ascended into heaven
and is seated at the right hand of the Father.
He will come again in glory to judge the living and
the dead,
and his kingdom will have no end.
We believe in the Holy Spirit, the Lord, the giver
of life,
who proceeds from the Father and the Son.
With the Father and the Son he is worshiped
and glorified.

REIKI AND CHRISTIAN BELIEFS: WHERE DO THEY INTERSECT?

He has spoken through the Prophets.
We believe in one holy catholic [read universal]
and apostolic Church.
We acknowledge one baptism for the forgiveness
of sins.
We look for the resurrection of the dead,
and the life of the world to come. Amen.

Church fathers researched Ancient Scripture along with biographies and letters from those who knew Jesus. They discussed their findings, and declared a belief in a Creator of the seen and "unseen". Unseen includes what is taking place in hands-on healing. When I am giving a Reiki session, I am praying for blessing and healing in the person's life, thankful for the positive affects this time spent together will bring.

So, where do Reiki and Christian beliefs intersect? The next few chapters address that topic.

7

WHERE REIKI AND CHRISTIAN BELIEFS INTERSECT

I believe there is a large common ground between the practice of Reiki, a hands-on healing modality, and New Testament Christian experiences.

After Jesus's resurrection the Holy –read "complete"- Spirit manifested in the early church during a season called Pentecost. The Apostle Paul wrote this about many spiritual gifts, manifestations of the Holy Spirit, in a letter to the church in Corinth:

> There are different kinds of gifts, but the same Spirit distributes them. There are different kinds of service, but the same Lord. There are different kinds of working, but

> in all of them and in everyone it is the same God at work.
>
> Now to each one the manifestation of the Spirit is given for the common good. To one there is given through the Spirit a message of wisdom, to another a message of knowledge by means of the same Spirit, to another faith by the same Spirit, **to another gifts of healing by that one Spirit**, to another miraculous powers, to another prophecy, to another distinguishing between spirits, to another speaking in different kinds of tongues, and to still another the interpretation of tongues. All these are the work of one and the same Spirit, and he distributes them to each one, just as he determines.
>
> 1 Corinthians 12: 4-11 (emphasis mine)

Paul shares the gift of healing is given by the Holy Spirit. Healing is not just for our own edification and empowerment. The full circle is complete when the person who has experienced healing, with a grateful heart, shares their experience to empower another who is on the same path; it is for the common good.

Here are other themes, or observations, I would like to carry forward in this and subsequent chapters:

- The parallels between the church practice of anointing with oil and Reiki
- Redemption—a form of healing—as a theme throughout the Bible
- Aaron's budding rod, an example of the Divine breathing life into that which is humanly dead; a form of healing
- Shifts in worship, from cultural identity and corporate worship (Old Testament) to individual identity, authenticity and responsibility (New Testament); Source of Life, the Being worthy of all worship—and the created, coming to a point of choosing worship
- Jesus's use of all modalities in teaching and healing
- Reiki and prayer
- The use of standing stones in ancient cultures to memorialize an important event
- Use of symbols as reminders, not objects with power
- Sharing our experiences of comfort or healing with others to give them hope

The following chapters provide more details to these points.

8

REIKI AND ANOINTING WITH OIL

Anointing with oil was an already established practice by the time James 5:14 was written. My father, an ordained minister, anointed me with oil once when I was very ill. Dad was trained to do so. It was neither the oil, nor the training that brought healing quickly back to my body. Dad used a religious method of saying, "I acknowledge something could be better in this situation and I'm a vessel relying on a greater Being to bring about change for good." Reiki is similar. Some would say Reiki is a newer label of an ancient practice of relying on Creator to intervene for the good of all.

An overarching theme of the Bible is a story of redemption being continually offered: Creator Being able and willing to put disjointed pieces together in a new, usable form with intricate beauty.

Redemption is also evidenced in Aaron's budding rod; the Source of Life breathing newness into that which is humanly dead. Are there areas of your life you want new life breathed into?

I use Reiki as a tool for supporting my desire to let go of old and bring in healthy, vibrant new growth in my life; redemption as a type of healing. Perhaps Reiki is a form of prayer: lots of thanksgiving and acknowledgment, some petitioning, and waiting in silence for transformation.

Transformation, no matter how subtle, inevitably occurs where our lives intersect with the Divine, with Source.

9

REIKI AND SOURCE OF HEALING

Christian healing history places God as the creator and great physician. Dr. Usui's practice of Reiki places Source as the center from which all healing flows. Connection to Source is connection to life, and as part of our lives, Creator set up systems to assist us in healing: physically, emotionally, socially, spiritually and mentally.

Reiki, like REM sleep, is something our Creator made as a tool to help us back to balance, if we choose. Critical processing and sometimes for me, reprocessing, takes place during REM sleep. Reiki is an active, awake way of allowing me to process, or reprocess, or actively, willingly let go of a burden. And I can choose to use Reiki at any point. I do not need to wait until I'm asleep. Jesus knew the restorative value of taking time away to refocus.

In my applied experience, being attuned to and practicing Holy Fire Reiki has only solidified and strengthen my understanding of God/Jesus/Holy Spirit, Creator Being, Source of Healing. Nicene Creed speaks of God being the Creator of all. Omnipresent. Omnipotent. No beginning. No ending. Redeemer. Healer.

There is another theme I see moving from Old Testament to New Testament; of moving from corporate everything to individual accountability and responsibility. Moses' version of worship in the Old Testament (acknowledging Creator's worthiness) appears to be very corporate, or community, driven. Paul's version of worship in the New Testament, after his encounter with the blinding light, moves towards individual accountability through the work of the Holy Spirit. Here the created moves to making the choice, the decision for individual worship.

I've also seen in my own life how learning to be accountable for me, including my health, has moved towards personal responsibility. Knowing and experiencing Reiki as a technique that can move my body towards balance and therefore health is not enough. I need to be using it. Like worship, or dental floss, knowledge without application does little good.

10

WHERE REIKI AND JESUS'S HEALING MINISTRY INTERSECT

Jesus used hands on healing. My favorite story is placed inside a story of Jesus on his way to heal a precious twelve year old daughter, only child of a prominent religious leader. It is of a woman with a dis-ease. Her tenacity to seek healing after twelve unrelenting years of unsuccessful treatment is remarkable. So is the distinction of types of touch.

Jesus is being pushed and shoved from all sides in the crowd, and yet He feels something different, unique in its transmission, when she touches the hem of his garment with faith and intention for a complete healing. She is immediately aware of healing in the shared moment when Jesus realized someone with a specific request reached out to Him. Here's the story inside the story in full, from Dr. Luke 8:41-56:

> Then a man named Jairus, a synagogue leader, came and fell at Jesus's feet, pleading with him to come to his house because his only daughter, a girl of about twelve, was dying.
>
> As Jesus was on his way, the crowds almost crushed him. And a woman was there who had been subject to bleeding for twelve years, but no one could heal her. She came up behind him and touched the edge of his cloak, and immediately her bleeding stopped.
>
> "Who touched me?" Jesus asked.
>
> When they all denied it, Peter said, "Master, the people are crowding and pressing against you."
>
> But Jesus said, "Someone touched me; I know that power has gone out from me."
>
> Then the woman, seeing that she could not go unnoticed, came trembling and fell at his feet. In the presence of all the people,

she told why she had touched him and how she had been instantly healed. Then he said to her, "Daughter, your faith has healed you. Go in peace."

While Jesus was still speaking, someone came from the house of Jairus, the synagogue leader. "Your daughter is dead," he said. "Don't bother the teacher anymore."

Hearing this, Jesus said to Jairus, "Don't be afraid; just believe, and she will be healed."

When he arrived at the house of Jairus, he did not let anyone go in with him except Peter, John and James, and the child's father and mother. Meanwhile, all the people were wailing and mourning for her. "Stop wailing," Jesus said. "She is not dead but asleep."

They laughed at him, knowing that she was dead. But he took her by the hand and said, "My child, get up!" Her spirit returned, and at once she stood up. Then Jesus told them to give her something to eat. Her parents were astonished, but he ordered them not to tell anyone what had happened.

The woman with the twelve year dis-ease was healed. The twelve year old daughter was also healed. Touch was used for both the prolonged, weary inducing ailment in an older body, and for a short, but critical, life-threating disease in a child.

Touch was not Jesus's only healing method. Jesus used multiple modalities to heal. Dr. Luke in 4:38 shares Jesus rebuked (used words) Simon's mother-in-law's fever. In Luke 5:17 he shares a story of Jesus using his words to heal a paralyzed man that his friends carried. These are the types of friends I love: they were all in when it came to helping their paralyzed friend. Seeing the house where Jesus was teaching was jam packed, they carried their friend up to the roof and secured him onto a gurney and lowered him by rope in front of Jesus. That rocks!

It is profound and interesting that the Greek base word from which we have our English words "salve" (ointment) and "salvation" literally translates "healing" or "wholeness". "Salvation" is a type of healing.

It appears to me that Jesus used touch primarily for two major reasons: blessing and healing. Children were being brought to him for blessing as seen in Matthew 19:13 and Mark 10:13. There are multiple written scenarios of Jesus touching to heal. Here are a few examples:

- Mark 6:5 a few sick people
- Mark 7:32 deaf man with a speech impediment
- Mark 8:23 blind man
- Luke 4:40 any who were ill with various diseases
- Luke 5:12 man full of leprosy
- Luke 13:13 woman with possible osteoporosis

Jesus used, as one of his modalities, touch for the purpose of blessing and hands-on healing. And I've seen firsthand that Reiki works to bring the body towards balance and heal itself.

Reiki always works for the greater good. Reiki always works. One does not need to be from a specific belief or in an altered state. Just as the unseen force of gravity has laws which govern it, the unseen Reiki, biofield, also has laws within which it works. Reiki cannot go where it is not wanted. Reiki can only work towards good. Like prayer.

11

WHERE REIKI, PRAYER AND SYMBOLS INTERSECT

Prayer is a universal language of a being seeking guidance, and relationship with I AM, and offering thanks. Sometimes it is a call for help, reiterating one's reliance. Reiki has energized my prayer life. I am significantly more thankful and my requests are deeper. As a result, prayer is more fulfilling. Reiki has prescribed hand placements, and I often use them when praying for someone.

I wasn't raised Catholic, but I think there is a correlation between the individual prayer beads on a rosary and whom or what the owner of the rosary beads is praying for or about. The Reiki hand placements is a physical guide for me as I pray over a situation or person. Rather than merely using words to ask I God/Jesus/Holy Spirit to help a friend, that petition is made more specific and covers a broader understanding for me through the use of kinesthetic movement.

Others used moving huge stones as an act of worship. Jacob (Genesis 28:18-21 and 35:14-15), Moses (Exodus 24:2-4) and Joshua (Joshua 4:2-9 and 24:27) each used standing stones of commemorate God/Jesus/Holy Spirit's intersection in their lives. Erecting standing stones was an ancient practice symbolizing something important, often spiritually, had occurred. It was a memory marker. Perhaps you collect specific keepsakes, rocks, or photographs as memory markers.

Another memory marker, or symbol, is prescribed in Exodus 28:17-21. The first High Priest, Aaron, was instructed to wear a breastplate that had specific gemstones identifying the unique twelve tribes of Israel.

Some Reiki lineages use rocks or gems as a tool. In Africa I recall dinner at an embassy personnel's home. In the entry they had a large bowl with gorgeous egg shaped rocks from all the places they had visited and lived. Then I look around my office. When Mike travels, sometimes he'll bring home a heart shaped rock for me. I love them. I don't worship them; that would be idolatry. But, like standing stones or gems in a breastplate, they are symbolic reminders.

And can symbols be analogies? Could believers be analogous to the Arc of the Covenant (Exodus 25:10-22)? A vessel (believer) containing structure (Ten Commandments), need for daily, fresh reliance on something greater (manna) and experiences with Creator continuing to demonstrate the ability to create new life in dead circumstances (Aaron's budding rod)? The writer of the book of Hebrews thought so (Hebrews 9:4).

12

REIKI AND KING DAVID'S DECLARATION

Shepherd boy turned king, David, wrote the song or Psalm 23. He begins by creating a picture of a place of healing, a place of calm serenity. It is a picture of a place to mirror in our own lives:

> The LORD is my shepherd, I lack nothing.
> He makes me lie down in green pastures,
> he leads me beside quiet waters,
> he refreshes my soul.
> He guides me along the right paths
> for his name's sake.
> Psalm 23:1-3

In our fast paced lives, we are being called to rest, to create spaces in our calendars for renewal. What if there is a practice of healing that could knock off the edges faster and help move your brain to a place of balanced quiet. Some are able to find solace (a form of healing) through working the twelve steps, or walking a prayer labyrinth. Others find calm and space through meditation, or hiking. Yoga is another option some find helpful as they seek to create space for calm, for healing. Let's open the conversation to include Reiki.

On the topic of healing, do I believe it is me, as a Reiki practitioner, that heals? No. I do believe Reiki helps the body relieve stress and encourages the natural healing process our Creator designed inside us.

Do I believe death means no healing occurred? Again, no. When my father, who was a nonsmoker, was diagnosed with terminal lung cancer of unknown origin, I began to wrestle with my beliefs in the afterlife.

What does complete healing mean? If I've been created by Source as an individualized manifestation of Source, then complete healing means being fully reconnected back into Source. For some reason, while on Earth, there is a spiritual vail I'm not privy to see through. Again from Apostle Paul's first letter to the Corinthians:

For now we see only a reflection as in a mirror; then we shall see face to face. Now I know in part; then I shall know fully, even as I am fully known.

I Corinthians 13:12

13

MORE OF WHERE REIKI AND CHRISTIAN BELIEFS INTERSECT

Here are other areas where I find Reiki and Christian beliefs share common ground:

- Knowing God/Jesus/Holy Spirit offers an individualized, intimate relationship
- Healing benefits of the daily practice of being connected to God/Jesus/Holy Spirit
- Daily reliance on God/Jesus/Holy Spirit for direction
- Petitioning God/Jesus/Holy Spirit for Peace to fill all the Earth
- Desiring goodwill towards people of different beliefs
- Quiet reflection is good for the created

- Allowing created to seek intuition/guidance from God/Jesus/Holy Spirit
- Acknowledging I am a created being in a world full of magnificence and wonder
- Use of prayer—thanksgiving for healing and blessing
- Reliance on spirit through God/Jesus/Holy Spirit, rather than ego

The list continues to grow as I continue to ask questions about where Reiki and Christian beliefs intersect. Part of my growth is leaning into the Apostle Paul's writing in his second letter to the Corinthians:

> Praise be to the God and Father of our Lord Jesus Christ, the Father of compassion and the God of all comfort, who comforts us in all our troubles, so that we can comfort those in any trouble with the comfort we ourselves receive from God.
>
> 2 Corinthians 1:3-4

Paul states that Creator is the source of comfort and comforts us. But my lessons learned in comforting are not for me alone. I was created to live community. My lessons need to be shared, so that others can see a different facet of the Creator, the Source of comfort and healing. For me, Reiki was a paradigm shift from what Jesus did two thousand years ago, to what Creator is still doing. Source is still in the business of healing.

PART THREE: REIKI CLAREMONT

...

14

ABOUT REIKI CLAREMONT
~AN INVITATION TO LEARN~

The purpose of Reiki Claremont is to create a safe space where people of all backgrounds and spiritual beliefs can learn about Reiki, a hands-on healing modality. Reiki can be a path for healing on all levels: spiritual, mental, emotional, physical, and social. Usui / Holy Fire II Reiki does this on a seemingly softer, gentler level, allowing for deeper healing.

Reiki Claremont currently offers:

~**Reiki Shares**: an opportunity for novice and experienced Reiki practitioners, alike, to gather and experience Reiki in a group setting where questions and observations are valued.

~**Reiki Talks with Meditations**: an opportunity to share what Reiki is about and demonstrate the power of self-care through quiet meditation.

~**Majestic Oak Tree Retreats: Reiki Integration**: personalized private retreats created for those interested in exploring how Reiki can do more by consciously focusing on the Reiki/spiritual aspects of life. We are, after all, spirit first and eternally.

~**Reiki classes of all levels:** Reiki I teaches the history and basics of noninvasive hand positions for a Reiki treatment, and includes a Reiki placement. Reiki II covers how to send Reiki to someone who is not in the room, much like intercessory prayer. During the Advanced Reiki Training (Reiki 3) one learns more about the biofield and how human energy works. Reiki Master training provides education on how to train others in Reiki.

~**Individual Reiki Sessions**: where clients experience Reiki's healing energy each month, or more often.

I encourage all, as part of their personal self-care routine, to create time to be still. To listen. To rejuvenate. Regular Reiki sessions are an integral part of my spiritual/mental/emotional/physical/social self-care.

You are invited to Reiki.

15

WHAT TO EXPECT IN A REIKI SESSION

Before having a Reiki session, or selecting a Reiki practitioner, it is wise to ask about the experience. Not all Reiki training is the same, nor as thorough. The Reiki practitioner should never diagnose, interfere with treatment plan from licensed medical professional, or touch in a manner that makes you feel uncomfortable—including placement of hands around the neck/chin area.

If this is your first Reiki session with me, I have you complete a brief questionnaire with an acknowledgement about what Reiki is and is not. You'll lay completely clothed (I encourage loose clothing for maximum comfort) on a massage table. I like to cover my clients with a sheet or blanket as often our body cools as we relax. I start with a silent prayer, being thankful for the healing and blessings you are about to receive and stating my desire for Reiki to flow and my ego to step aside. I explain that I'll be asking you to take a couple a deep breaths, and with your permission place my clean hands over your eyes, ears, on the top of your head, back of your head, shoulders (not too close to front of neck), arms, upper abdomen, mid abdomen, hips, knees, and feet. Additionally, there is a final, silent prayer of blessing. All of this takes close to an hour.

Sometimes clients fall asleep. Sometimes they feel a gush of emotions releasing and cry. Tears carry toxins, so it is great to get it all out. Most often the person on the massage table shares they feel relaxed.

After the session, I offer water. I encourage the person to make sure they are fully awake prior to driving or operating machinery. If this is their first session, I also share that I'll check in tomorrow. Sometimes, as the body moves towards balance, for people who have not been sleeping well, they can experience vivid dreams. I've only heard this feedback from people who have been quite stressed and just starting their self-care journey with Reiki. Most share they "slept like a rock."

Like the visual representation of a sound wave, sometimes when I'm practicing Reiki I can feel the gentle movement of a healthy biofield. There are times the biofield feels cold or silent in an area. I first noticed this with someone who needed knee replacement surgery. The energy around her hurt knee was cold at the beginning of a Reiki session. Following her sessions, she shared she felt less pain. Several clients have been mourning close, deep loss, or carrying heavy emotional burdens when they have come for a Reiki session. I often hear "Reiki is experiential"; they leave in a different, quieter place, and, like my personal Reiki session yesterday, went home and slept deeply.

Often people will ask how often they should schedule a routine appointment with a Reiki practitioner, even if they regularly practice Reiki on themselves. I encourage monthly appointments. It is easy to remember, and it supports the immeasurable idea of self-care.

I invite you to look for an Usui / Holy Fire II Reiki practitioner through the International Center for Reiki Training's (ICRT) Reiki Membership Association, or at ReikiMembership.com

I invite you to Reiki.

16

REIKI IN USE

In addition to complementing traditional health and wellness practices, how else can Reiki be used?

Since Reiki helps people move to a quieter, calmer place, the application is really only as limited as a person's imagination. Here are a few ways friends and practitioners have shared.

A recent Reiki trainee found sharing Reiki with her terminally ill friend decreased her friend's pain and nausea and increased her alertness in her final weeks. She is continuing to Reiki the family members through their deep loss.

■ ■ ■

Recently a friend asked for Reiki to be sent to her and the interview panel. She had lost her job due to cutbacks and had a few flat interviews. In this situation she was offered the job within 90 minutes of completing the interview. The job is exactly what she wanted and came with a substantial increase in pay.

■ ■ ■

One friend used Reiki to help her calmly assist her frustrated husband find his lost keys and wallet.

■ ■ ■

Another person I know is using Reiki to help navigate deep grief. The loss is still there, very personal, but Reiki is helping in the sleeping process. And as a result of better sleep, they are making healthier choices in the grieving process.

■ ■ ■

A friend is using Reiki as she reaches out to heal a deeply wounded relationship with a parent. It's helping her stay in the moment, find words in a calm manner and look for common ground to grow from.

■ ■ ■

Someone I know used Reiki to help calm herself and focus so she could drive herself to urgent care, as she was alone. It was her best urgent care experience ever, stitches and all.

■ ■ ■

A recent Reiki II graduate is using Reiki in her work. She is noticing clients being less agitated overall and more are falling asleep quickly during their procedures.

■ ■ ■

Reiki was used to assist in the process of purchasing a dream home. Through holding the space lightly, and waiting without demanding, events occurred and they got the home.

■ ■ ■

Another friend, in the midst of a large move, Reikied each part of the process: finding the new place with the right location and price, selling the current home with easy terms, deciding what to pack, give away, throw away, the movers, and the move. Moving was difficult because they were leaving friends, but a calmer experience because she used Reiki.

■ ■ ■

Several have used Reiki at their workspace: to prepare for the day, the clients, the space. In each situation, they report a calmer day, often reflecting on how they have changed since embracing Reiki.

■ ■ ■

Reiki has been sent to friends on the way to the hospital with very ill children: from easy access on the freeway and roads, to the admit staff, triage nurse, doctors, staff, appropriate room with necessary medicines available, correct diagnosis…

■ ■ ■

Reiki was sent to a friend starting a business. And to one selling a business.

■ ■ ■

A mom used when her youngest child left for college: for safety, right friendships and influences, challenging and fair professors…

■ ■ ■

Several friends I know use Reiki to prepare the space before they teach. They find the students (no matter the age) arrive more receptive to engage in the learning process.

■ ■ ■

I used meditative walks in the wilderness next to our home, prayer and Reiki to write and edit this book. I was able to easily write the manuscripts for three books and create outlines for four workshops in seven weeks. That's a new, personal record. My last book, <u>Incongruent</u>, an unpublished manuscript, took several years, after the initial inspirational poem.

■ ■ ■

Reiki is used in times of crisis, as a supplication. It can also be used as a form of a blessing:

- For the great adventures someone will have on their trip
- For celebrations of all types
- For lifelong union before a wedding
- Before shopping for, or giving the "perfect" gift
- For transportation
- For transformation
- For new experiences that will be validating and encouraging
- For plans, including the start of a new year

PART FOUR: MY ROAD TO USUI / HOLY FIRE II REIKI

...

17

WHAT'S IN A NAME?

What's in a Name? When I was pregnant with my daughter, many asked if we had names picked out. Mike and I had a list going, but hadn't decided. A friend gave us their copy of a names book that had traditional meanings listed after the names. I don't recall the name of the book, but we had hours of fun putting names together. Mike, my sister Sandra and I even created sets of names that would, we thought, help people to stop asking. When the baby was born, we'd have a name, right?

The doctor was fairly certain our baby would be a girl. We wanted to honor our mothers and decided on Helen Elaine. When running this by Mike's eldest sister, she quickly shared that we'd be naming the baby the same name for "Light" in two languages, Greek and French. We went back to the drawing board.

We finally decided on Morgan Elaine, meaning "Light on the edge of the water or sea" or "Lighthouse". As brand new, but significantly older parents at any birthing class we took, we wanted her name to symbolize our desire for her life. We wanted hers to be a life full of choices for Good, for Light, for Life. When she was born, it seemed to suit her.

The Ancient Hebrews, descendants from Abraham and Sarai, also wanted to a create a relevant name—for their Creator. They mulled over what to call Source, Life giver, Protector, Provider… They agreed the name should never be spoken as they were mere mortals in comparison. The tetragrammaton "YHWH" is one of the commonly used names of Creator God used in the Hebrew Bible. It is most often seen written as "Yahweh" or "The Lord."

Mike's name means "watchful, vigilant Guardian Archangel". His parents used the name "Michael" for two of their five boys. It must have had a significant meaning to them, especially as Irish Catholics. My name means "Dwelling/Home/Castle of a Princess." It's taken me a long time to grow into the "Princess" part. It's not that I didn't like the idea of being special. I have a physical birth defect, a clef lip. Before I was born, I was protected.

18

PROTECTED!

My parents, Doug and Elaine Crowder, were United Methodist missionaries in the Democratic Republic of Congo, Africa. About a year after they married (1957), they moved to Congo and worked at their first assignment as teachers for children of missionaries. About a year later, my oldest sister, Sandra was born.

Things were unraveling politically in Congo. After World War II, the European powers divided the continent of Africa by geographical boundaries. Big mountain. Huge river... You get the idea. What they did not take into consideration were the ancient tribal boundaries. A massive tribe had been divided in the countries of Angola and Congo. In addition to the stressful political angst, communication to America through mail took weeks, and phone service was available from only the capitol and one other major city.

As political unrest grew in the early 1960s, my parents, with Sandra, fled Congo to present day Zimbabwe in a United Nations transport. While refugees, my sister Anna was born. My parent's large Samsonite suitcase served as her first crib: one side of the suitcase for the tiny newborn, the other for clean, cloth diapers.

Following this evacuation, my parents spent time in Belgium for proper language training in French. As they kept up with their intensive language studies, they also kept an ear open to the events in their now beloved Congo. President Mabutu had come to power in a bloodless coup, but things were very fluid as tribes jockeyed for positions of power and influence. Being careful not to have another child during this time of flux and political strife, you can imagine their surprise when Mom was told she was pregnant with me.

They returned to Africa as planned, and went to an annual gathering with other national and expatriate leaders in central Congo. While at Wembo Nyama, word came that the rebels were outside of town. The missionary men were not to leave, but the women and children were allowed to go. Mom and Dad celebrated their 7th anniversary with Dad baking Mom his traditional anniversary cake, and the next day they said their goodbyes as Dad was held hostage and Mom, pregnant with me, along with Sandra, Anna and the other women and children once again loaded onto a United Nations DC-10 to head to safety.

While Dad was held captive for weeks with other men, he was taken out to be shot, but wasn't. As the story is so well told in Virginia Law's <u>Appointment Congo</u>, her mission pilot husband, Burleigh Law, was not at Wembo Nyama with his mission plane when the rebels arrived, and was not taken hostage. Daily he listened to reports and wanted to help the men. He flew over in his small mission plane over the Wembo Nyama airstrip and dropped a bottle with a message. The rebel in charge of the dirt air strip signaled Burleigh permission to land. When he landed, a rebel with a different agenda, shot Burleigh Law.

The hostages, including my Dad, were allowed to try to save his life. "Uncle Doctor" Hewlit did everything possible, but they were not able to save Burleigh Law. Just days after burying him in a simple wooden hand-made casket, the rebels released all the hostages.

I can only imagine the stress my Mom endured each day, culminating in Burleigh's death days before Dad was released.

The Congolese school year was late getting started due to the rebel activities, but the Congolese were determined to get a full year of education completed, and everyone was trying to reestablish a new norm after the crisis.

Mom's due date with me was early January. As my family needed to fly to the mission station with a small hospital and general family doctor, they left Sandoa. There were students who were waiting for my Dad's return and there were finals to give. Daily Mom would go for a long walk hoping to induce labor. For weeks she walked, and waited and finally, three weeks later I was born. Dad was in the delivery room when Dr. Devon Corbet helped my Mom deliver me. It was too much after ALL they had endured: an unexpected pregnancy, being taken hostage, Burleigh's death, and now, me with a clef lip.

Doctor Devon's words were wise and calming from the beginning. "Now before the weeds start to grow," he began. He shared that he didn't know why there weren't more babies born with clef lips and offered a medical leave for my parents to fly to America, or South Africa, for plastic surgery for me. After I demonstrated I could nurse without issue, they opted to wait for the infant anesthesiologist to come to Congo eight months later.

This is the foundation for why I am certain I am forever loved by the Creator. He chose the timing and place of my birth, protected my unborn life during months of unnerving stress. My clef lip reminds me, when I remember to look at it, that my Dad was protected throughout the hostage experience, allowing me to have an earthly father to raise me.

King David's poetry has deep meaning for me.

> "For you created my inmost being; you knit me together in my mother's womb. I praise you because I am fearfully and wonderfully made; your works are wonderful, I know that full well. My frame was not hidden from you when I was made in the secret place, when I was woven together in the depths of the earth. Your eyes saw my unformed body; all the days ordained for me were written in your book before one of them came to be. How precious to me are your thoughts, God! How vast is the sum of them! Were I to count them, they would outnumber the grains of sand—when I awake, I am still with you."

Psalm 139 verses 13-18

In this song or poem, King David shares the Creator is bigger than my mind can conceive, yet pays attention to every detail. I agree with the Ancient Hebrews.

Is there a Name for such a Being, Life's Source?

Is there more in this Creator's "vastness" regarding healing for us, now, than we've been willing to accept in our collective Judeo Christian belief system?

19

THE BOOK CLUB

In 2010 my friend Beth Misner asked me to join a newly forming book club. During one conversation about a section of a book we'd read, the practice of meditation came up. I asked about how to meditate successfully—perhaps I should insert here how I'd meditated: six pieces of blank paper and pen or pencil ready to capture every idea my brain shared, in, at times, desperate hope, my brain would quiet and I could be at peace. So, when my "meditating" time was up, I'd have grocery lists, summer to-do lists, people to write Thank You notes to... you get the idea! My brain had acted more like a freight train of ideas, than a peaceful place. When I asked about how to mediate successfully, I was seriously looking for answers! I wanted to get to that quiet, calm, peace-filled space.

As an undergraduate student, one of my professors was interested in hypnosis. At the end of class one day, we were invited to stay, if we wished (and sign a consent form), to experience hypnosis as a group. I found the experience fascinating as I was aware of my surroundings the entire time and came from it refreshed, energized, focused. I used that as my base line for what meditating could feel like.

Janice Berkenheger, a fellow book club participant, listened to my questions and offered to share Reiki with me as a way to quiet my brain. We set up a fifteen minute session in a private room in her Pilates studio. I sat in a chair focusing on my breathing. I was aware she had her hands quietly on my head, neck and shoulders. By the end of the session I felt different. It physically felt like my brain had shifted from primarily using one side, to accessing both sides. For me, this was a calmer, better perspective or place from which to make decisions. When she offered her next beginning class, I joined.

20

HOLY FIRE II REIKI

After practicing Reiki for a few years, I read about a softer, gentler style of Reiki William Lee Rand, and others, were teaching: Usui / Holy Fire II Reiki. I was interested in training with William and his class "just so happened" to coincide with a pre-existing family vacation. Mike urged me to go. To honor my African upbringing, I opted to Airb-n-b a tree house without electricity or running water. It's a story for another time, but in its own way, very healing!

Reiki training with nine others and William in his Lemurio Round House in Hana, Maui, was an exceptional experience. The natural beauty and serenity of the area matched the beauty and serenity of Holy Fire Reiki.

Back on the mainland it was easy to sign up for the advanced classes. Although I am a Reiki master in two lineages, I choose to use and teach Usui / Holy Fire II Reiki due to its softer, gentler and effective healing properties. I am currently a Professional Member of the International Center for Reiki Training (ICRT) Reiki Membership Association.

The Reiki lineages I am trained in uses four levels of Reiki. Reiki I teaches the history and basics of noninvasive hand positions for a Reiki treatment, and includes a Reiki placement. Reiki II covers how to send Reiki to someone who is not in the room, much like intercessory prayer. During the Advanced Reiki Training one learns more about the biofield. Reiki master training provides education on how to train others in Reiki. My knowledge of Reiki and respect for I AM, Abundant Source, definitely grew through the process in both lineages.

21

HOW DID MY REIKI PLACEMENT CHANGE ME?

Immediately following my Reiki placement, or attunement, I became aware of great peace inside my usually active mind. That was significant for me! Additionally, I found a gentle sense of space, between my palms when I held them about 4 inches apart in front of me and gratefully thought of being connected to Source.

When I thought back to a time when my father, an ordained minister, poured oil on my head when I was really ill, and held his hands there, I realized Reiki was not my first experience with hands-on healing. The Reiki attunement was different in that there was training, but I imagine my dad was trained in what to say prior to pouring oil and praying over me.

There is a meditation that has had a profound effect on me. It is a grounding mediation. One where you imagine yourself like an old tree with deep roots going into the ground, deeper than the underground streams, deep, deep into the earth, and then, you are guided to move your thoughts to the moon and far, far beyond. It was when I was thinking about how vast the galaxy is that I had this experience of being more connected with Creator, Source, I AM, than I had ever experienced prior AND that Creator is vastly unfathomable. I am deeply thankful for that experience.

When experiencing the ignition process of Usui / Holy Fire igniting the flame, symbolic of the relationship to Holy Fire as a Usui / Holy Fire II master, I became increasingly mindful of my need for healing while simultaneously experiencing deep wounds no longer having a hold over my life. It was as if the roots had disappeared; deep healing for sure.

I've also seen on multiple occasions, one must be willing to let go of the pain to heal. Sometimes one has morphed their identity into the brokenness of the experience or situation. Part of the healing process can be to begin to paint a mental image of what you could look like without that pain. Yes, it can be the unknown, but when the pain of staying where you are is greater than taking a step into the unknown of healing, most often one chooses to take the step towards healing. (Yes, I am a glass half full believer.)

In my Reiki journey, I've come to understand others see the world differently, really differently. I'm not speaking of political or social views. I mean literally. I have friends who see colors around people, depending on what the person is concentrating on. I know people who are guided intuitively, or who hear words of healing to share. The Bible talks about Christians belonging to One body, but having different skill sets to work together to keep the Body of Christ strong. Being in the Holy Fire Reiki world has offered opportunities for me to see how creative God is. It is humbling and beautiful.

PART FIVE: CONCLUSION IN TWO PARTS

...

22

CONCLUSION

I believe there is a deepening need for individuals who want to change their world (sphere of influence)—spiritually, socially, emotionally, mentally, physically—to be caring for themselves. This is not a call for selfish indulgence. It is a call to create spaces to intentionally connect with Source.

I have desired in our time together to create a protected space—based on a solid spiritual foundation, surrounded and walled by experiences—where we can have a conversation about a hands-on healing modality, Reiki. I am opening a dialogue. If this conversation causes you to consider, then act on, ways to destress, pursue healing, create a personal space for quiet reflection, or engage in a new modality for a conversation with the Divine, then I will consider our time spent together highly beneficial.

May you be deeply blessed on your journey, so that you may then gratefully light the way for another.

You are already doing just that. Your purchase of this book is helping to support the building of the Mama Lynn Center in Kindu, Democratic Republic of Congo. This project, under the leadership and watchful eye of Bishop Unda Yemba Gabriel, will support the healing of women, and their families, who have survived the atrocities of tribal conflict, war and personal devastation. A minimum of ten percent of the proceeds of this book you are reading are donated. Thank you!

You are already lighting the path of healing for others. I celebrate with you!

Sending Reiki with love and blessings,

Sarah

23

WHAT'S NEXT?

<u>*Reiki and Christian Beliefs: Where Do They Intersect?*</u> is the first in a series "Reiki and …" by Sarah C. Stockham.

When I first sat to write, following a long walk in Johnson's Pasture, Mother's Day 2016, I envisioned one book. But in the writing and editing process it became clear my initial thoughts were, in reality, several books. Currently I have working manuscripts for <u>*Reiki and Chakras*</u>, and <u>*Reiki and Goal Setting*</u>. I am concurrently working on workshops for both books.

Made in the USA
Coppell, TX
25 July 2020